Unfinished Art of Life &

More Than That

SARATHPRATHAP S

Made with ♥ on the Notion Press Platform

www.notionpress.com

Dedication

I like to dedicate one and all which are present and all which lived in this world. Though I have some special mention too.

As I have mentioned in the previous book, I learned most of my life with the movies so when I enter into day-to-day life with people, I feel a gap between the cinematic version of myself and the world. But still movies are wonderful teachers for me. So, I like to dedicate this book to Abbas Kiarostami, an Iranian film director, screenwriter, poet, photographer, and film producer. More or less, he gave me a chance of hope to live, through Taste of cherry and showed me the world from a different angle, one is filled with love and humanity. I just wonder how much he would have gone through or what kind of life he lived, to make those films.

I would also like to dedicate this Book to Director Pa.Ranjith, an Indian film director, producer and screenwriter who primarily works in Tamil cinema and to Director Mari Selvaraj, an Indian film director and screenwriter who works in the Tamil film industry. I always had this thought like life has two separate phases: personal and social. But when I saw movies from these directors, I felt that personal and social are interconnected and I get inspiration from them to speak 'what I want to speak', 'From where I want to speak', 'How I want to speak'. They serve as elder brothers guiding me, the younger one, towards the future.

Dedication

*I would also like to dedicate this book to
Dr. Tholkappiyan Thirumavalavan, a political leader, scholar
and activist from the southern Indian state of Tamil Nadu. He
is a Member of Parliament from Chidambaram, and the
Leader and President of Viduthalai Chiruthaigal Katchi. He
serves as a teacher to me in both political and life. Whenever
I get confused about where to begin addressing an issue, he
offers a viewpoint from which I can fully analyse and
understand it.*

*I would also like to dedicate this book to
Babasaheb Dr.B.R. Ambedkar, an Indian jurist, economist,
social reformer and political leader who chaired the
committee that drafted the Constitution of India based on the
debates of the Constituent Assembly. The more I come to
know about you, the more I realise: when I was thinking
about you I find myself falling in love with your vision of the
world.*

*I would also like to dedicate this book to my parents, family,
teachers, and friends.*

*I would also like to dedicate my current colleagues especially
for giving me the experience of the world, for being there and
for helping me.*

Thank you one and all.

Preface

In this section I like to add 2 dialogues, one from the speech of Director Pa. Ranjith that is

> *"We all have love and care*
> *with everyone*
> *I see my cinema as a tool to*
> *register those*
> *happiness and issues faced in*
> *daily life"*

Next one is from Thors from the Vinland saga anime that is

> *"You don't have enemies,*
> *The truth is…*
> *nobody has them.*
> *Nobody in this entire world*
> *deserves to get hurt"*

So, I also see my book as expression of life, filled with love and tried to speak about the issues in life and more than that.

Acknowledgements

I have this thought that helping is not only about sharing someone's hardship, but also about simply being there.

So, I would like to thank everyone and everything that is part of my life, the world and space around me.

I sent my last book for printing in a rush, so I made mistakes in it. I hope I've corrected them this time. In that book, I thanked ChatGPT, but I was actually using Microsoft Copilot. This time, I'm using ChatGPT to correct my grammatical errors in English.

The flower graphics I used are from the app or website CANVA it has been a great help, and I also the use Inshot app mostly for photo editing

♣ தேவையற்ற நேரத்தில்
பொழியும் உன்மேல்
வன்மத்தை உமிழ்கிறேன்,
இதுவரை உன்னை ரசித்ததாய்
ஞாபகமில்லை!
தேவையான நேரத்தில்
பொழியும் உன்னை
கொண்டாடும் எனக்கு,
ஏனோ நெகிழியினுள் வாழும் மக்களை
என் மனம் சந்திக்கவில்லை!

♣ ஒன்னுமே செய்யவேனாம்
அவன் எனக்கு புல்லனு
இருந்தா போதும்

நீ வளத்தியேடி
எந்த மக்க உன்ன பாக்குது

♣ *When Arnheid asked Thorfinn,*
"Why should I live?"
I had no answer, like Thorfinn.
Hope one day I will answer her

♣ *If you ask about our friendship,*
I don't text you
I don't call you
I don't even visit you
Maybe in the future, too.
But for sure,
I will treasure the moments we had,
And I imagine visiting you, though

♣ *Hope,*
The path I pushed you on is beautiful,
But I still regret pushing you, though

♣ *Sister asked,*
"Aren't you happy about publishing?"
"Yeah, I'm happy,
But I loved the progress more than that"

♣ *Why does white colour dress*
make us feel pure and good?

♣ *In the end,*
it's always "Questions".
But why!?
Maybe, is this life!?
Searching for answers

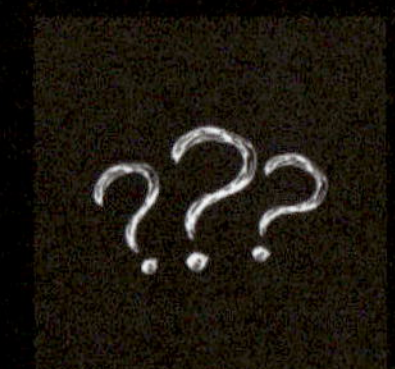

♣ *Thank you, Zero Two*
For reminding me that I too can love

♣ உதவி செய்ய பெயர்கள் தேவையா!?

♣ அவளால் நானும்,
அவளும் நானும்,
அவளும் நானும்,
அவளும் நானும்,
அவளும் நானும்,
அவளால் நானும்

♣ அன்றோ சனிக்கிழமை
வீட்டில் காகம் கரைந்தால்
எழவு விழும் என்று
காகத்தை நோக்கி கல் எறிந்தனர்
எனக்கோ
எழவு விழுந்தாலும் பரவாயில்லை
என்று கேட்டு ரசித்தேன் காகத்தின் கூக்குரலை
ஏனெனில் பள்ளிக்கு அன்று எனக்கு விடுப்பு
வேண்டும் பின்னர் தான் தெரிந்தது
காகங்கள் பேசிக் கொள்வதை பார்த்து
கல் எறிந்துள்ளனர் என்று

♣ வெகு தூரம் போனாலும்
உனை தேடி வருவேன் வெகுளியாய்
தொலை தூரம் போனாலும்
தொலைபேசியில் உனை பார்ப்பேன்
அருகில் இருந்தாலும்
அடக்கமாக இருப்பேன் அன்பே

♣ *It just makes me smile*
When you tried to take a glance
When I was teaching her
Hope that spark ignited between us as a bond

♣ *You won't know*
What you did to other people
Until and unless they express it to you

♣ சொ(செ)ல்லா காதல்!

♣ *You are the one who asked reasons!*
But why you are not listening now!?
Is it too late!?
Or you don't need the reasons between us?

♣ *Am I being stubborn?*
Am I being emotionally reserved!?
Am I being subtle!?
when it comes to expressing myself

Stubborn?
Emotionally reserved?
Subtle?
I think it's just my way of expressing myself

♣ *I thought I'll give a comeback in my life*
But the greatest comeback in my life is "You"

♣ *Dear Abbas Kiarostami,*
The movies you directed
aren't just movies for me
They look like life
Thanks for that
And I am showing mine now

♣ ஏனோ தெரியவில்லை!
எல்லோரிலும் உனை காண்கிறேன்
ஏனோ தெரியவில்லையா!?
அது *pattern recognition* ஆக இருக்கலாம்

♣ *I understand the hurt*
Which my actions create
at least somehow, I guess
At the same time
I don't want to end my life
With saying sorry to people
I'll meet
There are still a lot in the queue, though

♣ பலத்தை ஆதிக்கத்திற்கு பயன்படுத்தாத வரையில்,
அது பலவீனத்திற்கு பலமே,
எனினும்,
மக்களுக்கான விடுதலையின் போது
மக்கள் பக்கம் நிற்பதே தேவையானது,
ஏனெனில் நாமெல்லாம் மக்கள்

♣ மக்களுக்காகதான் அரசியலே தவிர,
அரசியலுக்காக மக்கள் இல்லை

♣ *Again, I realize!*
I wrote,
I've realized I needed you
When I came out of the house,
But inside the house,
I had a piece of your presence

♣ *Almost, I can see no happiness*
For "Winner winner chicken dinner"
All I can see is only domination
In the name of satisfaction

♣ *I like the beauty*

♣ *I was somewhere else!*
Somewhere my heart felt light
OH! A dream

♣ *I tell myself*
to Attend your marriage
with happiness and
Experience that time too
Just like I did all over my life

♣ *It's okay*
Laugh, sing
Dance, mourn
Cry, smile
Make a movie
Live in that
Live out of that
Just live

♣ *Nothing is poetic*
Everything is poetic
Something is poetic
Little bit is poetic
And so you and me are poetic

♣ *A friend posted my poem*
As I have belief in the movie "Certified Copy"
I don't like to claim it as mine
It's just yours
I'm happy that you shared your emotions

♣ *About the past:*
Even if I get the time travel machine
I don't want to use it
I don't want the drama of my life to fade

♣ *Hope you are well*
Don't take me wrong
For not reaching out to you
It's just, I don't know
What you are going through!
As Usual, Any help!?

♣ *We shout*
We bow
We smile
We jump
Towards life
Life, life
Life, life
I am the life

♣ *Games are meant to pause*
when needed
In that way,
I don't like Unpausable games now

♣ எப்படி உள்ளதோ உன் தோற்றம்
பார்த்து நாளாகிவிட்டது தோழனே, தோழியே

♣ ஆழமான உணர்வுகளையும்
ஆர்ப்பரிக்கும் உணர்வுகளையும்
தமிழில் விவரிக்கிறேன்
அது இயல்புதானே
ஏனெனில் என் தாய்மொழி தமிழ்
இருப்பினும் செழிப்பு மற்றும்
ஒடுக்குமுறைகளுக்கு அப்பாற்பட்டு
மொழியை தொடர்பு கொள்ள பயன்படுத்தும்
ஒரு கருவியாக பார்க்கிறேன்

♣ எழுதா கவிதை இது!
என்னவென்று தெரியா கவிதை இது!
ஆனால் ஏதோ ஒன்று
உனை நோக்கி எனை இழுத்தது!

♣ நானும் வாழ்கிறேன்
நாடக வாழ்க்கை!

♣ வியக்கிறேன்,
ஒரு பெண் குழந்தையின் பார்வையில்
தந்தை என்னவென்று
வியக்கிறேன்,
ஒரு தாத்தாவின் பார்வையில்
பேரகுழந்தையின் பந்தம் எப்படி படுத்தென்று

♣ *Once I wrote you and me are poetic*
But why do I prioritize "you"
When the scale is between you and me?

♣ *I hope, at least for now*
I'm fine with living in the memories of us

♣ *Sometimes I check*
the remaining time on movies
To see when it's gonna end
Sometimes I check
because I don't want it to end

♣ *You haven't expressed*
what I did to you
So I can never know until you do
But when I recall,
All I can recall is the hurt I gave you

♣ *I like it,*
When my mom shouts at my father
It's not about dominating,
It's about breaking the stereotypes of
media, culture, and religion

♣ *: Why do you write this?*
: Who do you write for?
: Do I have to answer these questions
*   to write?*
: No, it's just my question

♣ *The more and more I dig my emotions*
It's just endless sorry

♣ மூடினு சாப்புட்ரா,
அமைதியா சாப்புட்ரா,
சாப்பிடும்போது பேசாத,
சாப்புட்ரா கம்முனு

♣ *In my mind*
I never stop talking

♣ தற்கொலையை,
ஒரு மனிதருக்கு நம்பிக்கை தராத
சமுகத்தின் கொலையாகவே பார்க்கிறேன்

♣ காதல் வயப்பட்டேன் என எண்ணினேன்
இல்லை!
என்மீது உள்ள காதலை
படங்களின் வழியாக
உன்மீது திணித்துள்ளேன்

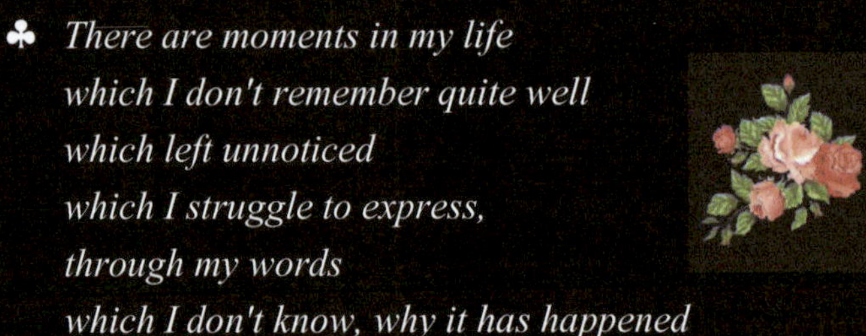

♣ *There are moments in my life*
which I don't remember quite well
which left unnoticed
which I struggle to express,
through my words
which I don't know, why it has happened

♣ *I don't remember*
why I decided to publish,
or what pushed me to publish
But I remember,
I thought to show what life is
from someone's POV

♣ *A typo poem:*
If you like someone,
you will get better at it

♣ *I never expected*
That giving the published book
to a family member
would earn me the lovely moment
I haven't had in my lifetime until now

♣ *What am I doing!?*
Just getting comfortable
with the present
When the past meets present,
I'm done

♣ என்னவென்று தெரியா கவிதை நாம்
எங்குபோய் சொல்வேன் இந்த உணர்வுகளை
வாழ்வின் இறுதிவரை
பொக்கிஷமாய் வைக்க இருக்கிறேன்

♣ *Most of the time,*
I feel like calling someone,
even after a long time for my need
then I won't call
until I get a need.
And my friend once told me,
Need is what makes
humans communicate with each other.
Maybe there is something
which may even stop despite the need

♣ *I too got bored,*
by hearing the same story of
going to school every time
when we have a talk
with my father
But this time I wondered,
what makes people
repeat the same story again and again?

♣ *New fear unlocked:*
I thought I shouldn't hurt others
for my curiosity by my questions
But what if!?
Every question I ask
Hurts others!?

♣ *Sorry Mamma, Sorry Pappa,*
I don't know how to express it,
maybe it'll hurt you,
obviously it will,
because it hurts for me

♣ *Thank you both*
For crying about my stubbornness

♣ உனக்கு புரியவே புரியாதா?

♣ *: Sorry, Apo life nah enaku enanuh therla*
: Apo ipo?

♣ *Who do you write for!?*
Why do you write for!?
How do you write for!?
I see it as a mirror and a reminder, mostly

♣ *Film is a collection of thoughts and life*

♣ *In the name of safety and power*
it makes me laugh about border on earth

♣ *For me life looks like Puzzles and*
Questions based om that

♣ *I am always at the past*
From there,
where I see the present and future

♣ *Even I haven't known your name*
I love the way you are
You will be with me
You will be remembered

♣ *You live*
You live in my words
You live in my book

You live in my memory
You will never die
It's just I lack the memory to recall you

♣ *I hope we both have cried about the same thing*

♣ *Wish I could go with Frieren*
to the Phantoms of the Dead,
People are still alive though

♣ *I wonder,*
How much joy, they would have had!

♣ *STAY*
Stay in my life
To the very end

♣ *At least for you people*
It's not about my comfort
It's about the people
who didn't give up on me,
And the people whom I don't want to give up

♣ *I like to ask*
or maybe tell!
We are gonna die soon
so, what's stopping you?
Are you scared!?
the world isn't same always!
the world is same always!
the hope and love is there,
and so, the remaining too!
Face it

♣ அறம் செய்வோம்
மனிதத்தை திரட்டி
எல்லாவற்றிற்குமான உலகிற்காக

♣ When it all comes to light
Will I live?
I doubt it, the race is cold

♣ : Do you love?
: Yeah
: What is love then!?
: Maybe, agreeing with assumptions!
: Define it,
  without defining how do you love?
: No, I don't want to
: Okay then, keep an eye over
  stereotypes, harm, and unrealistic expectations
  in the name of love

♣ Maybe... Not Maybe!
Of course, I played too many games
And drawn parallels between People and levels, I think

♣ At least after that moment
I don't remember
Me enjoying with you
Without her

♣ Memory gets blur day by day
Once I did it purposely,
and now it got inverse

♣ *Swirl of regrets, Yoon Jin-seo*

♣ *Tasukete! Tasukete!*
Tasukete! Tasukete!
Tasukete! Tasukete!
Tasukete! Tasukete!
Tasukete! Tasukete!

♣ *If someone asks me,*
How do you plan to live
Like Askeladd asked Thorfinn
Obviously! I don't know
And yeah, like you, like many,
I too got dreams
% Though the reality isn't the same
But I know, I can help others
From what I have
I know that can make a change
That can make love
To you, to me

♣ *Hey, Abbas Kiarostami*
I saw a scene from your movie
in my life
That moment is beautiful
Their life is hard though
Maybe I ain't noticing other scenes in my life
For now I like to say, I miss you

♣ *What will you do?*
When war comes upon us!
Will you go to a safe place?
Is there a Vinland in our world!?
Why am I not talking about war?
Why aren't the deaths of people affecting us?
Why are we not caring about
Iran-Israel
Russia-Ukraine
Hamas-Israel
Myanmar
Middle East
Africa
Mexico
Pakistan

♣ *You are not alone*
You have more or less 8,204,700,023 people
to help you
Take care

♣ அமைதியின் ரூபமே போராட்டம்

♣ *Is it me!?*
Or is it your home!?
Which stops me from calling you

♣ You didn't give up on me!
Why I should!?
So, if someone does,
will you too!?
I don't know,
But I don't want to!

♣ Taking advantage of the situation
In the name of emotion
May lead to guilt,
Because you may meet the people
Moral and Morality along the way

♣ An undefined emotion
Still a puzzle for humans and it will be.
A key of unity
Love!
Happy Valentine's Day

♣ I have a superstitious belief,
That I'll die after the day
I full-heartedly dance in the rain

♣ I can't write anything
more than Love and Pain
Some people may consider
Pain as part of Love,
Yeah, I too
But sometimes it's distinct

♣ *No wonder I made my first movie*
  After watching Jao Nok Krajok (Mundane History)

♣ *Dance, Sing, Write, Read,*
  Blah, Blah, Blah…
  We almost have everything in us, naturally

♣ *: Who's that person,*
  whom you always talk to!?
  who asks you questions in your poems!?
  : It's just me and Myself

♣ *: Do you trust them!?*
  you won't! that easily
  probably you never done
  yeah, seriously when have you even
  done something like that
  you just manipulate

♣ *I hope one day the 'truuh truuh' will end*
  And then I will hear your voice
  Which will give me happiness
  Then we can have a conversation

♣ *The lamb lives in sanctuary inside the fence*

♣ *These hopes make me*
  laugh, blush, feel idiotic, ironic,
  That a girl will propose to me
  Haha… How lazy I am

♣ *I am going to die without knowing the answers*
I can only assume answers
Do I have to assume?
I don't think so
Let's die without knowing the answers
What's wrong in that!? :)

♣ *As a younger one,*
I don't understand elder ones.
As an elder one,
I don't understand younger ones.
As a friend,
I don't understand other friends.
As a non-lover,
I don't understand what love is.
As a male,
I don't understand females.
As a Human,
I don't understand other living beings.
As a student,
I don't understand teachers.
As a teacher,
I don't understand students.
As I,
I don't understand you.
I know understanding is about
Assumption, connection, and willingness to change.
But I'm afraid to assume something
Which I don't know about.
So better tell me what you feel
So, I can at least assume

♣ *Erasing history*
Pushes us into a blank space
Where we won't have any reminder
For looking back

♣ *Who or what are you working for*
Yourself?
People around you?
Humanity?
The world?
Beyond the world?
God?
Non-existence?
Pride?

♣ *What is the use of hiding things in poetry*
If your reader can't identify it
Why are you doing it?
Own satisfaction?
Yearning for the spotlight?
Afraid of finding out?
I wish they would find
It's just, I expect a little bit of effort from them,
And also, things you said)))

♣ *I'm afraid of you*
why do you put me into this pain?
I also have another view about you

♣ புயல் கரையை கடக்கும் வரை
காத்திருப்பது நன்று
எல்லா நேரத்திலும்,
எல்லோரும் அதை கடைப்பிடிக்க வேண்டியதில்லை
புயல் கரையை கடக்கும் வரை
காத்திருக்க வேண்டிய அவசியமில்லை
எல்லா நேரத்திலும்,
எல்லோராலும் அதை ஏற்றுக்கொள்ள முடியதில்லை

♣ *Young and Anxious*
Funny and Dreams
Romantic and Platonic
Gomen and Rogue
Dark and Night
Bright and Sun

♣ *We may be some unique freaks,*
and I'm fine with our way, mostly
But I think they don't deserve our
'Blank ha vitutu pogura habit'
In my case,
I'm afraid of causing and getting hurt
I don't know what yours is!
So once, why once!? Twice, thrice—
rethink as many times as you want, mapla

♣ *If I treat anyone kindly,*
You are the one who comes to mind,
As the reason

♣ *Why do you learn how to be kind?*
To treat others with kindness?
Nah, I am asking about you!
Usually, you do things for yourself
So why!?
Maybe I can forgive myself someday

♣ *The past can't be changed,*
but old people ain't the past

♣ *I made sure people remember me,*
But in a miserable way, I guess!

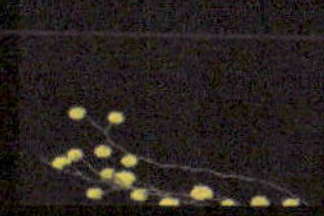

♣ *I started watching a movie.*
I was expecting a scene,
Which influenced me to download that movie.
Until the very end,
That scene never came.
I realized I had downloaded another movie instead.
The movie was fine, though.
It's Poetry (2010)

♣ *You said we all are beauty,*
So why haven't you loved me?
It's just me—
I haven't got the heart and the knowledge of beauty to love
you.
I repeat,
You are beautiful

♣ I don't have belief in God.
I believe in the efforts of people.
I seek someone while mourning.
Mostly, I won't have someone.
So, I seek something.
Maybe that's why people pray, I guess.
But God ain't "just God" here.
It's full of belief, superstition, and hierarchy.
You could say, "You can just have belief in God."
But I think if I do,
I will eventually drown in the same pond

♣ புதிதாய் எனைப் பார்க்கிறேன்

♣ Do art should have meaning behind that?
Why it can't be meaningless!
Of course it can be

♣ Why does the world believe that,
they can simply pay off
those they have wronged—
rather than taking responsibility
You may pay off their financial need,
But you can never pay off their emotional bond

♣ Why does she have to have—
this much impact on me!?

♣ *Only the name of discrimination is changing*
  The form is never changing!
  So, work towards the change of form 
  rather than the name

♣ *After watching Arnheid*
  in Viland saga anime I get a question
  How do those people continue to live!?

♣ *Of course,*
  it's our efforts,
  but opportunity—also has a part in it
  (Note: This is not to be turned against reservation.)

♣ *When watching movies,*
  I feel like I should stop talking with people
  And drown in the imaginations

♣ *'Oh my GOD'*
  I seriously hate the usage of this word
  Yet I convince myself, and I like to say
  I don't like the way this word's usage
  is deeply ingrained in our mind as a casual one

♣ *How can I mourn for others!?* 

♣ *The depth of 'Don't waste your time' is balancing priorities*

♣ *I wanted to let you go,*
But why was I trying to make you understand me!?
I remember—
I wanted to show
I ain't any fictional character—

But is that real!?

♣ *I feel like,*
I don't have even the small rights
to get angry at someone
who refuse to help me
even whatever the situation I am in
I am asking help
so they have every right to deny it

♣ *It's nothing,*
it's something,
It's often everything,
but it's still many things—
The stages of our thinking in learning something

♣ *As players,*
we all have a certain position in the game.
It's okay to make a move in a play,
But we must associate again
To face the next one

♣ *Why do I have to forget her!?*
She ain't the promise I made to others
All I felt was happy with her

♣ *After repeatedly watching*
Thors from Vinland Saga,
I like to ask,
'Why should self-defence include attacking back!?

♣ *I guess,*
one of the peak moments of happiness
for elders is—
seeing the younger ones achieve
what they desired, failed at, or couldn't reach

♣ *The more I observe,*
The more I realize
How far away I am
from understanding people

♣ *How can I avoid elders if I want a better world!?*

♣ *The hero inside me isn't dead yet*
I suppose he is the cruel part in there

♣ *Ahhh! What a geez I am*
Who doesn't know how to enjoy with people,
on their way.
Urusei, Bakayaro!
Come out of your imaginary world first,
And see how others suffer

♣ *I couldn't learn,*
Because I was so much of myself.
I learn by myself,
Because people give me opportunity

♣ *In that moment,*
you will learn the wrath of your actions
Better learn it before, baka!

♣ *Our minds,*
become the blender of need, emotion, and logic
When we are struck

♣ *We know clearly*
Where we are,
What we are up to
But still, the reason
We cling
Is because we are afraid
Of taking risks,
The weight of losing,
And the blindness of influence

♣ *Indian constitution is not something,*
which is formed up not to hurt others alone
it is also built up to prevent ourselves
from hurting

♣ *I haven't observed males much on this—*
Not in general, but I have seen a few females
They don't want to leave anyone behind,
Whoever it is, whatever they are to them.
I admire it if it's their own choice.
But why!? Dear Femalehood

♣ *Everyone has kindness in them*
Our work is to bring out that

♣ *A little empathy toward others*
can bring out kindness
Because everyone has kindness in them

♣ *I go far from you,*
Whenever I take a sip of reality.
I can see it
I am just repeating—
You, the people, movies, games,
Emotions I felt, actions I did,
Imaginations I get.
There is nothing there
More than this
Even if I can write, I don't want to—

♣ *I wonder,*
What you—
Did to me!

♣ *A sword is not just one made of steel*
There are other forms too

♣ *Can I love and unlove—*
someone at the same time!?

♣ *If you worked today,*
then you've earned the right to eat.
சாப்ட சாப்பாடுக்கு படிக்கனும்
வேலையே ஆவுல, அதுக்குள்ள சோறா?
செய்றதுக்கு ஒரு வேலை,
அப்பறம் மூணு வேலை சோறு.
நீ என்ன வேலை பாத்துக் கிழிச்சிட்ட,
உனக்கு இப்ப சோறு கேக்குது?
இந்த பொழப்பு பாத்து,
சோறு திங்கறதுக்கு பட்டினி கடந்து சாகலாம்.
சோறு ஒன்னுதான் கேடு இதுக்கு
திங்குற சோத்துக்கு ஏதாவது வேலை செய்றியா?
நீ செய்யுறது ஒரு வேலை,
இதுக்கு வேல, வேலைக்கு சோறு

♣ *They give life to countless children every season*
Even many of them give life to countless children every day
They feed them daily with all their soul
They nourish them every now and then
Their life tends to mix with their children
There comes a time—
When their full-grown children clash with the world
I hope it's enough to make them happy
What a loser I am!?
To stay out of or miss out on this wonderful cycle

♣ *I wonder,*
whether I still stick to my thought—
"I can't speak, cry, laugh, or fight with a dead body,
so, I don't have to see the person after death."
At least until now, in expectations.
Why does my world
change upside down—
when it comes to you!?

♣ *You can see the form of discrimination,*
whenever it is about minority and majority.
Not all forms of discrimination
exist in numbers, though

♣ *The way to order*
differs between people
But the nuances of difference—
are filled with love.
Especially power—
it is born from love,
but it has its own limit.
Love is inclusive,
and all other forms are exclusive

♣ *Aren't you tired!?*
you haven't stopped running still!
from what you're
where do you plan to?
—don't know

♣ *There is nothing wrong with people*
who use power or strength to create order
they just follow what they believe,
and what they have been taught or learned.
They just don't realize
that they may end up the same.
We just have to help them—
by the empathy of love

♣ *I wonder how the meet will be!*
every day I learn something
every day my mind changes its view on something
still running though!

♣ *I am looking for flowers,*
but the plants also seem beautiful.
I guess I am looking for beauty, though.
I was looking for knowledge,
but procrastination also seems beautiful.
I guess I am looking for a degree, though.
Haha, seeing flowers without stems
manipulating knowledge without understanding
feels incomplete

♣ *Movies without subtitles are fine—*
studies with intuition are fine—
but depth needs subtitles in learning, though

♣ *You kill numerous times—*
people in your mind.
Still, how can you feel when they really die!?

♣ *Okāsan, Otōsan—*
In life, I made the decisions for me,
even though you may have pushed sometimes.
There is a part of me accepting it,
so please don't have regrets.
I am seeing the beauty out there because of you

♣ *The reality is far—*
crueller and more beautiful
than my imaginations
Maybe that's the life which is far

♣ *I look people from far*
when I get close to them
I see everyone lives in drama genre

♣ *We wait outside for the storm to pass,*
or we step inside the storm.
We don't know
whether it's better to wait or walk through.
Either in or out,
we are stuck with the storm

♣ *One who knows what love is—*
Finds it everywhere, or nowhere at all.
When it's about him,
He has always been a puzzle

♣ *Someone who fits nowhere*
Someone who thinks to unite all

♣ *When I miss something,*
I look back in the history!
But what if history isn't there?
Haha, maybe YouTube history

♣ *Can't you see we are burning!?—*
The line is mostly set as
Either hero vs. villain or
God vs. Asura/Satan
In the politics of India

♣ *Ahh, It's over*
The contradictory days
The sky is always clear—
but the attraction ain't
Oh welcome, my dear friend— again

♣ *Let the pain heal you—*

♣ *It's taking me years*
To catch up with you, Ishu
Hope—
You could be here
I could've talked
...To whom am I writing these!?
I don't even attend funerals

♣ உன்னுடைய இருப்பை
எல்லோரும் விருக்கப் போவதில்லை,
எனவே, அந்த ஒரு நம்பிக்கைக்காக வாழ்

♣ *What are you!?*
Being there—
Just being there—
I am just learning—
Learning—and learning—
My puzzle is so lovely,
Further and further—
when it keeps unfolding!

♣ கேள்வி நீ, பதிலும் நீ
கேள்வி நான், பதிலும் நான்
கேள்வி நீங்கள், பதிலும் நீங்கள்
கேள்வி நாங்கள், பதிலும் நாங்கள் 
கேள்வி நாம், பதிலும் நாம்

♣ *As they have introduced us to technology—*
Make sure you don't leave them behind

♣ *Colours are from nature*

♣ *Still, I don't get what is LGBTQIA+*
But I'm learning to support.
why need completeness,
If I can care even now?
caring, at its depth,
Is space for all

♣ *Unexpectedly,*
I am happy that,
The poems I wrote have become
Meaningless!

♣ *History has been colonized*
So, dig more—
to rewrite it
through etymology
and political archaeology

♣ *Revolution is much farther*
and more intense than Agitation
That's why he said
Educate, Agitate, Organize

♣ வாழ்,
வாழ்க்கை உனக்கு கேள்விகளாக தெரியும்
வாழ்க்கை உனக்கு புதிர்களாக தெரியும்
ஆனாலும் வாழ்
உனது பதில்களின் தேடலை நிறுத்தாதே
நீ செல்லும் பாதையில்
அழகாய்,
உன் முன் தன்னை வெளிப்படுத்தும்
பதில்கள்!

♣ *The older people projected in movies*
You may see it as innocence
But I see it as Injustice
Vulnerability done to a citizen
By government and people
because of the gap between people and law

♣ *Maybe I haven't got the courage*
to express directly
so, I use Art

♣ *There is a difference between*
  All are equal before the law and
  The law is equal for all
  Article 14 and Article 44

♣ *Minds of people don't follow*
  Coulomb's law always.
  Sometimes they attract the same,
  sometimes the opposite —

♣ *I wish to exist*
  as bit of hope
  which can stop people from
  hating the world completely

Here are some words for you to create your own poems.
I have created one with these words as base,
here it is:

    Throughout history, war destroyed identity
      but not the love

I hope you will also start expressing yourself from here.

www.ingramcontent.com/pod-product-compliance
Lightning Source LLC
Chambersburg PA
CBHW040917110726
48005CB00006B/924